Little Spills

and Other Poems I Cannot Contain

Little Spills

and Other Poems I Cannot Contain

Poems and Photographs by
KYRA FREEMAN

REDHAWK
PUBLICATIONS

Dedicated to the people of Walden.

Table of Contents

Foreword
Page 1

Introduction
Page 5

Walden History Timeline
Page 9

Chapter 1
The Prehistory—Indians Reign Supreme
(Time Immemorial to 1820 A.D.)
Page 19

Chapter 2
Exploration, Trapping, and Hunting
(1820 to 1870)
Page 27

Chapter 3
Early White Settlement (1870-1880)
Page 37

Chapter 4
Mining and the Founding of Walden
(1880 to 1890)
Page 45

Chapter 5
The Origins of the Cattle Ranching Domain
(Late 1800s)
Page 53

Chapter 6
Early Twentieth Century in Walden
(1900-1920)
Page 71

Chapter 7
The Local Employment/Industries:
Government, Education, Mining, Timber,
Gas and Oil, Railroad, Retail,
Outdoor Recreation, and Tourism
Page 85

Chapter 8
The Future of Walden: Assumptions, New
Trends, and Potential
Page 97

Afterword
Page 111

Acknowledgments
Page 115

Notes
Page 117

Suggested Reading
Page 127

List of Walden's Mayors
Page 128

Foreword

For we writers and historians, it would probably be easier to write a history of Athens, Greece, than to write about the history of a small town in America. Athens has been around for about twenty-five hundred years and, for a time, sat at the center of western civilization.

Not so much for a small town in Jackson County, Colorado, which is still designated as frontier because we have less than one inhabitant per square mile.

I once mentioned in a speech that it's unusual for a small town such as Walden, Colorado, to get any national notice unless that town experiences a mass murder or a natural disaster. But small towns do have their own unique narratives, the kind of stories that I would call intimate history.

I don't know if Walden has had, or ever will have, an impact on the world, and I don't know if we'd want that. As you read through *Back to Walden,* you'll see this area, by virtue of its altitude and location, attracted some pretty tough and independent characters, not all of whom stayed. Walden isn't Sun Valley; it's hard to live in this high mountain valley, where temperatures will reach minus thirty degrees at least once each winter. Even the American Indians who frequented North Park for four hundred years got the heck out when winter came along.

There were no monumental battles fought here, although a few of the early settlers learned that if some heavily armed Ute Indians suggested you leave the valley, you probably should leave the valley. No great political movements started here, no uber-famous people were born here, and our most influential river, the Platte, in terms of its contributions to the great Midwestern waterways, may have been given its name because of a typological error.

You'll find in these pages that a lot of intimate history is also charming history. In Walden's first mayoral election, eleven votes were cast. One of our first public buildings cost $45 to construct. An inordinate number of immigrants to this high, dry, cold mountain valley came from hot and humid Missouri.

Author Bob Romero starts each chapter with a quote from Henry David Thoreau, who, as every educated student used to know, wound his philosophy around his seasons at Walden Pond in Massachusetts. Thoreau never visited Walden, Colorado, and the naming of the town had nothing to do with that small lake.

Then again, you can't find the tranquil isolation Thoreau enjoyed at Walden Pond anymore. The 1.7-mile track around that lake is one of the most heavily traveled walking trails in the state.

But you can capture that feeling in Walden, Colorado, and thanks to Bob Romero for reminding us how we got to where we are, and why we still choose to be here.

Jim Dustin, Mayor
Walden, Colorado
March 15, 2021

Introduction

This is the story and history of a small rural town in the north central Colorado Rocky Mountains.

Walden, Colorado, was settled and incorporated on December 2, 1890, by hardy and resilient Americans looking for opportunity while moving westward from the Midwestern, Eastern, and Southern states. There were also a good number of recently arrived immigrants, primarily from European countries. These early North Park pioneers first tried hunting and mining to support themselves and their families but then quickly turned to cattle ranching for their livelihood. They staked out their land and water claims and began raising Hereford and Shorthorn cattle, some Texas Longhorns, and eventually some sheep in a high, well-watered mountain park that had once been the basin of a shallow sea. The tall native grasses that grew abundantly on the river-bottom meadows provided the feed for their livestock.

But these settlers in the early 1880s were not the first people to occupy the high, wide-open park. Almost certainly, the Paleo Indians had passed through the area thousands of years earlier to hunt megafauna. More recently the Plains tribes—which included the Arapaho, the Cheyenne, and, primarily, the Ute tribe—hunted bison there for about 400 years prior to the arrival of the whites. The park was still teeming with a variety of wildlife when the free-spirited American mountain men began trapping beaver in the 1820s. Later in the 1800s, a variety of wildlife—bison, deer, elk, antelope, wolves, grizzly bears, mountain lions (wildcats), and sage hen—were still found there in great abundance. (Bison were mistakenly called buffalo, and the name stuck. But they are not considered buffalo. They are their own species, unique to North America and the northern reaches of Mexico.)

The area was still very isolated in the 1880s; and because of the severe winters, North Park was one of the last places to be permanently settled in the area that became the territory of Colorado in 1861 and the state of Colorado in 1876, exactly one hundred years after the United States became a country. The nomadic Indians used the Park primarily as their summer hunting grounds, and they would depart for lower, warmer climes for the frigid winters. In 1880, when the Utes were forced onto the Uintah Reservation, the white settlers moved in and began in earnest building their homesteads and cattle ranches. They began living in the Park year round. Walden as a town became the "Hub of the Park" and served as the cattle rancher's supply point in a very convenient, centrally located site at the confluence of two rivers.

Timeline of Significant Events in the History of Walden

PREHISTORY
Time Immemorial to 1995 A.D.

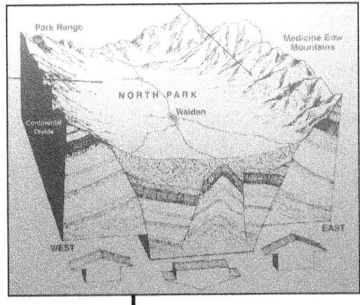

The current site of Walden, Colorado, was located at the bottom of a shallow sea in an intermountain glacial basin that now encompasses what is known as North Park.

45 million years ago   **1400s-1800s A.D.**

Nomadic Native Americans, which included the Arapaho, Cheyenne, and principally the Ute tribes, occupied North Park and used the area around Walden as their summer hunting ground.

1858 A.D.
Denver – "Queen City of the Plains," as it was known then, or the "Mile High City," as it is known now – was founded and would become the future capital of the State of Colorado, in 1876.

1881 A.D.
On Feb. 28, 1881, Marcus Aurelius Walden, as the first postmaster, established a Walden Post Office.

| 1858 | 1884 | 1881 |

1884 A.D.
One year after he had arrived in 1883, civil engineer Ike Greene, the true founder of the Town of Walden, built a house on a "homestead of 160 acres on the Illinois River," where the Town of Walden is now located.

1885 A.D.
Construction began on the first Walden school building, at the Forest Service station site. The school was dedicated in 1891.

1885　1886　　　　　1887

1886 A.D.
Ike Greene donated 20 acres to be used as a community cemetery when his third child, Ivan, died.

1887 A.D.
The first child born in Walden, Alice Shippey married and lived in Denver for most of her life.

1888 A.D.
The first store, C.E. Mosman General Merchandise, was established by C.E. "Gene" Mosman. It became the supply point for the entire North Park and made Walden the "Hub of the Park."

| 1888 | 1890 |

1890 A.D.
On December 2, Walden was incorporated as a municipality in the State of Colorado. The population was still 64. Walden was the second town in North Park; Teller City (1881) had been the first.

1891 A.D.
Gene Mosman became the first mayor of Walden on March 2, 1891.

1901 A.D.
The first bank in Walden, North Park Bank, was started by Francis E. Milner.

1891 — **1901** — **1904**

1904 A.D.
The first firehouse was built by E.F. Loffer for the Town for $60. The first true public waterworks were started when $14,000 in water bonds were issued to supply water to the Town of Walden.

1911 A.D.
The coming of the railroad happened on October 25, 1911, dubbed as "Railroad Day." A railroad line was built from Laramie, Wyoming, bringing great hopes for a new era of prosperity and growth in Walden and North Park.

| 1911 | 1912-13 |

1912-13 A.D.
The august Jackson County courthouse was built for $28,000 using sandstone from Walden Hill, north of the Michigan River, and native limestone from a quarry on the Mendenhall Ranch.

1913 A.D.
The *Jackson County Star* was founded by Art Wilkens. The *Star* celebrated its 100-year anniversary in 2013.

1995 A.D.
The Walden Wetlands were established in concert with the Lions Club.

1941-45 A.D.
On December 7, 1941, the Japanese attacked Pearl Harbor and the United States entered World War II. Many men and some women left Walden to serve their country, and much of the mail received from soldiers was published in The *Jackson County Star*.

CHAPTER 1

The Prehistory: Indians Reign Supreme
(Time Immemorial to 1820 A.D.)

"The universe is wider than our view of it."
— Henry David Thoreau

History is an interpretation of a record of significant events, and prehistory is a branch of knowledge about what conceivably happened before historical events were being written down for posterity. We depend on archeological artifacts such as arrowheads and shark teeth, for instance, in an attempt to determine what occurred during an earlier time period. History is based on the written word. Walden, like most communities, has both a written history and a prehistory to research, study, and document.

In addition, we, as individuals and our communities, have a past, a present, and a future. Individuals generally tend to focus on the present day, and perhaps this is the best approach as a popular bit of wisdom advises that one should live a little bit in the past, a little bit in the future, and take advantage of the present moment. Another adage states that we study the past to better understand the present, so we can plan for the future. These three goals are incorporated in this book.

Henry David Thoreau, author of the American classic *Walden*, believed that we should "toe the line" of the present, but he also wrote, "The universe is wider than our view of it." This is true in terms of both time and space as there is so much more of the world than what we see in front of us. The land, the landforms, and the landscape also have a past.

This is apt for the story of the geological past and the natural environment around Walden, Colorado. Geologists hypothesize that during the Cretaceous Period, the central United States was part of a shoreline that repeatedly advanced and retreated. About seventy million years ago, the land mass rose and created the present landforms in Colorado. Approximately fifty-three million years ago, the 10,000- to 12,000-foot mountains that encircle the town of Walden were being uplifted as part of the Rocky Mountains.[1] At some point in time, in what is now known as North Park, the Park basin, or the floor, dropped suddenly and flattened out at about an 8,000-foot elevation.

About forty-three million years ago, an enormous amount of water collected in the basin, and the current site of Walden was then located at the bottom of a shallow sea. Similarly, other Colorado mountain parks or valleys—such as the San Luis Valley, South Park, and Middle Park—were created. The San Luis Valley is the largest of these geological landforms, and, as a result, it contains the enormous Great Sand Dunes, formed when a large body of water, Alamosa Lake, overflowed and then drained southward into New Mexico; the windblown sand collected in one part of the valley.[2] North Park is smaller in size, but in a similar situation two dunes were formed there. Thus, North Park can claim the north and south sand dunes.

In his epic book, Thoreau speculates as to how Walden Pond in Concord, Massachusetts, was created. The legend that he refers to is as follows:

"...anciently the Indians were holding a pow-wow upon a hill here, which rose as high into the heavens as the pond now sinks deep into the earth, and they used much profanity, as the story goes, though this vice is one of which the Indians were never guilty, and while they were thus engaged the hill shook and suddenly sank, and only one squaw, named Walden, escaped, and from her the pond was named."[3]

Walden, Colorado, though, was named for Marcus Aurelius Walden. Walden Pond in Concord, Massachusetts, was thought to be bottomless, as has been speculated about some of the ponds around Walden, Colorado. Although this is not true, the Walden ponds, similar to the Concord pond, are "without any visible inlet or outlet except by the clouds and evaporation."[4] This author grew up and played in and around

 these wetlands that were formally named and established as the "Walden Wetlands" by the town and the Lions Club in 1995.

In any case, the area around Walden is indeed well watered, and the entire North Park is one of the best watered areas in all of Colorado. The North Platte with its three forks is the major river. The Illinois and Michigan rivers come together in a junction north of Walden. Numerous other tributaries and creeks throughout the Park run full during the spring and summer, and "water the area more thoroughly than any of the other Colorado mountain parks."[5]

Archeologists who study past human life as revealed by relics left by ancient people tell us that the big-game hunters known as Paleo Indians hunted mammoth and other megafauna in North Park about nine thousand to thirteen thousand years ago. The flaked spear points that have been found extensively in the vicinity provide the evidence of this early activity.[6]

Archeologists also state that a continuous stream of indigenous people hunted large bison in the area. Later, the smaller bison were hunted for some four hundred years by the nomadic Indians that included the Ute, Arapaho, and Cheyenne. The bison were hunted first on foot and then, by the late 1600s, on horseback.

Those horses were acquired from the Spaniards, who transported them by boat from Europe to Mexico and then to North America, in what is known today as the Southwest region of the United States, beginning in the 1500s. The horse then gradually moved northward into the hands of the mountain and plains Indians. As the Native Americans acquired the horse, they developed a highly skilled equestrian culture that made them more mobile, and this became advantageous for hunting bison. North Park, because of the abundance of bison, became the primary hunting grounds of the Northern Ute Indians. The area around Walden particularly was known as the summer hunting grounds of the Indians.

The Indians were still hunting the bison throughout most of the 1800s in North

Park. But in the early part of the 19th century, the sunset of the prehistory period had arrived, and the sunrise of a new time period was on the horizon when the Europeans entered North Park in the 1820s. The mountain men and explorers began writing down and recording what they did and what they experienced in and around Walden, and this was the beginning of written history in North Park.

CHAPTER 2

Exploration, Trapping, and Hunting
(1820 to 1870)

"For what reason have I this vast range and circuit, some square miles of unfrequented forest, for my privacy, abandoned to me by men?"
— HENRY DAVID THOREAU

In the early 1820s, North Park was still a wildlife paradise. The area had extensive mountains and forest surrounding the Park and was teeming with wildlife of all types. North Park would later in the century become known as one of the great hunting grounds of the nation. The area was still very isolated in the early nineteenth century. The Indians were still present during the summer and fall, but North Park was virtually abandoned by man in the winter and spring.

This was about to change.

The Spanish Conquistadors, the first Europeans in the area, explored into the Southwest beginning in 1540. They settled in New Mexico by 1598; in Santa Fe by 1610; and at Taos Pueblo, which today is the oldest town in the entire United States, by 1615. The existing Taos Pueblo structures date to about 1350 A.D.,[1] with continuous habitation at the same location. During Spanish colonization, the Spaniards traveled as far north as Nebraska in the 1720 Villasur Expedition to the Platte River. In 1776, during the Dominguez/Escalante Expedition, they explored throughout the Western Slope of Colorado and into Utah, but not into North Park.

In 1821, Mexico won its independence from Spain, and the southwestern area of North America became part of Mexico. It would remain so until 1848, when the area that now comprises the states of California, New Mexico, Arizona, and parts of Nevada, Utah, and Colorado became territories of the United States. Texas had won its independence from Mexico in 1836 and was an independent nation state for ten years, until it was annexed by the United States in 1845.

It was in the 1820s, though, that Europeans first visited North Park, initially for beaver trapping, then for hunting, and intermittently for mining. Some of the early mountain men were French-Canadians, but later they were of all nationalities.

Mountain man Peg Leg Smith amputated his own leg while trapping beaver in North Park near Walden. He was taken in by the Ute Indians who helped heal his wound. Eventually, he was carried out on a "litter between two horses" by fellow trappers. Smith later whittled his own wooden leg and lived out his life as "legendary as any."[2] The leader of another trapping party in North Park in 1827 was Sylvestre Pratte, who became ill and was probably the first European to die in the Park.

Kit Carson, who had settled in Taos, New Mexico, in 1826, was in North Park in 1831 trapping beaver.[3] He was also a regular at Bent's Fort, in La Junta, Colorado, as were other trappers and mountain men such as Ceran St. Vrain, who was also in North Park in 1827.

In 1844, John Fremont (Pathfinder) entered North Park from the north and traversed through the entire Park, exiting at the southern end and describing it in glowing terms. He wrote the following narrative:

The valley narrowed as we ascended and presently divided into a gorge, through which the river passed on as through a gate. A beautiful circular valley of 40 miles in diameter, walled in all around with snowy mountains, rich with water and game, ringed with pines on the mountain sides below the snow, and a paradise to all grazing animals.[4]

In 1846, a gold strike was made on Independence Mountain, which in all likelihood was triggered by information obtained as a result of the Fremont Expedition.[5] This mine was again being worked later in 1870, when the so-called "Independence Mountain Massacre" happened. In that event, twenty white miners who were placer mining for gold on "Ute land without permission" were killed. As the story goes, the chief of the Ute Mountain Utes, Chief Colorow, gave the miners "three sleeps to get out or be killed."[6] When the Utes came back a few days later, on July 4, 1870, they killed all the men. The only response was that the U.S. Cavalry came in and buried the dead and left. This was an unfortunate and tragic event in North Park history. While it was the first serious attempt at mining in the Park, it would not be the last.

By the early 1850s, the Spanish settlements from northern New Mexico moved north into what is today southern Colorado. San Luis, Colorado, which is less than 200 miles south of Walden as the crow flies, was founded in 1852 and is today the oldest town in Colorado. By 1858, Denver was founded; and in 1861, Colorado became a territory created by the U.S. Congress. In the process, some parts of southern Colorado that until then had been part of the Territory of New Mexico, formed in 1850, became part of Colorado. In 1876 Colorado was accepted as a state in the Union, with Denver as the state capital.

Hunting for food was imperative for survival in North Park. Beaver trapping, though, was the lure for many of the trappers and mountain men. The tall beaver-skin hat became fashionable in the East, which increased the demand for beaver pelts. But beaver did not make for very good eating, so the availability of all the other wildlife in North Park was a godsend for the rugged mountain men.

Bison was the dominant species that occupied the North Park "Bullpen." During the summer, it was the bull bison that grazed the meadows. The mountain bison were a subgroup unto themselves, and they lived more or less permanently in the mountainous parts of the Park. The bulls that grazed on the tall, lush grass in the Park would leave in the fall to begin the rut, thus mixing with the female bison in the plains outside the Park.[7] Elk, deer, bighorn sheep, and antelope all competed for the lush grazing. The Park was a balanced ecosystem of natural wildlife, with both predators—which included eagles, hawks, bobcats, mountain lions (wildcats), wolves, and grizzly bears—and their prey, which included diverse types of rabbits, ducks, and prairie dogs.

The cycle of life was omnipotent and ever-present. The iron law of life for the wild animals in North Park was, "Nothing in nature gets out of life alive."[8]

The Indians were dependent primarily on the bison, and the entire ecosystem was fragile but in sync. After communal bison hunts, they would butcher the animals, and the jerking of the meat would be done by all members of the clan or tribe. They made good use of all parts of the animal. They dried, cured, and preserved the meat, which was essential for the survival of all members of the tribe during the hard, cold winter that was dead certain to come.

The European explorers who entered the Park faced the same dilemma as the Indians. They learned "still hunting" methods from the Indians, and they did not make much of a dent on the numbers of the great herds of bison grazing in the Park.[9]

Bison were still plentiful when the homesteader and cattleman moved into the Park in the late 1870s to early 1880s. The death knell for the bison, however, sounded when the world supply of leather declined and bison hides became valuable as a commodity. The infamous "hide hunters" moved in and decimated the bison, not just in North Park, but throughout the western United States. This ecological disaster happened in less than a decade, between 1875 and 1883, in concert with the forced removal of the Northern Utes to the Uintah Reservation in northeastern Utah. These events occurred after the "Meeker Massacre" of 1879 and the subsequent Ute Removal Act of 1880. The white Europeans moved into Colorado en masse and firmly established themselves in North Park.

It is commonplace to assign cause and effect to simultaneous historical events, but the other reality is that life and history are cyclical. When one cycle ends, another begins, and this at least to some degree is what happened in North Park. One group (Native Americans) that was dependent on a particular resource (bison) and a certain lifestyle (moving and hunting) were removed, and another group (white Europeans) moved in to fill the vacuum.

The question that has arisen, in the moral and historical context, is did these events happen by design as some have charged? In other words, were the bison slaughtered in order to force out the Indians? Or did these simultaneous events happen randomly? The debate as to which scenario transpired back in the nineteenth century is a never-ending argument, as is much of history. The reality for North Park and the history of Walden is that the next time period had emerged. This would now be the beginning of permanent year-round settlement and human presence in North Park and Walden. The hub of the Park was about to be launched, and the area would no longer be routinely abandoned by man.

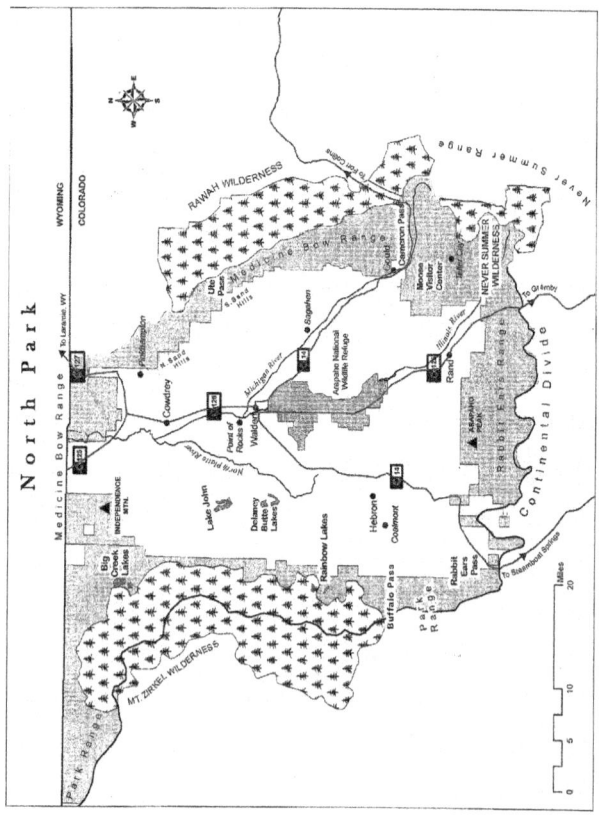

CHAPTER 3

Early White Settlement
(1870 to 1880)

"In any weather, at any hour of the day or night, I have been anxious to improve the nick of time, and notch it on my stick too; to stand on the meeting of two eternities, the past and future, which is precisely the present moment; to toe that line."

— HENRY DAVID THOREAU

In 1876 Colorado became a state, formed from the area that had been established as the Colorado Territory in 1861. Since the onset of American sovereignty in the Southwest in 1848, and, before that, the Louisiana Purchase in 1803, the Western states had been experiencing the gradual arrival and the continuing occupation by European Americans. The forces of "manifest destiny" were essentially being implemented in the westward expansion of the

United States, from the Atlantic Ocean to the Pacific Ocean.

A big part of the reason for the changes taking place had to do with the differing perceptions of land use and ownership. For the Native Americans who were on the land, their perception was that they did not own the land. In a sense at least from their point of view, they were owned by the land. They routinely occupied numerous sites for a short time but then moved on without making permanent settlement or leaving much of a footprint.

For the white Europeans, however, occupation of land meant ownership; and to establish ownership, the land had to be claimed, plotted, and surveyed. So as the Americans moved westward land was being surveyed and then shortly thereafter it was claimed, developed, and worked.

In 1874, U.S. government surveyors worked in North Park to complete the United States Geological Survey (USGS).[1] The land still legally belonged to the Utes, according to a treaty negotiated with the U.S. government.[2] But technically, as a result of the Louisiana Purchase in 1803 and the redrawing of national borders that occurred at the end of the Mexican American War in 1848, the land was also part of the United States and the Colorado Territory.

Canadian James Pinkham, who had served as a scout and a guide for the U.S. government surveyors, returned to North Park on June 12, 1875. He began building a block house the following year, which then became a road ranch known as Pinkhampton, in the "neck of the Park."[3]

Pinkham had originally arrived in the Park in the early 1870s. He had left his family in Canada in 1868, then worked building railroads through Illinois, Michigan, and Iowa. He then moved to Laramie, Wyoming, and regularly traveled into North Park and became a trapper, prospector, and hermit. According to one description, he was "hardy of nature and rustic of habit." Pinkham lived to be ninety, and there is no evidence that he ever became a naturalized citizen of the United States.[4]

When the government surveyors came into North Park, Pinkham accompanied them and helped them name the Park's creeks and rivers. Thus, we have Pinkham Creek at Kings Canyon, and the Michigan and Illinois rivers merged near what would become the town of Walden. The naming of the Michigan River and the Illinois River had nothing to do with any connection between North Park and these states other than that Pinkham had previously lived and worked in these states. It is uncertain how the Platte River was named, although the question arises: Was it supposed to be the Pratte River for Sylvestre Pratte, the first European to die in North Park in 1827?

August Speck, born in Germany on September 24, 1831, moved into the Park three days after Pinkham. He moved into the southern end and also helped the surveyors name some of the streams there, such as Willow Creek. He also was a hunter and prospector, and eventually a rancher. He lived out his life in North Park around Owl Ridge and Teller City. He died in 1920 at the age of eighty-nine, also, apparently, never having become a naturalized citizen of the United States.[5]

In 1876, Colorado became the 38th state in the Union. That same year, early efforts were made to build a road, called North Park Road, from Laramie, Wyoming. This would certify the northern end of the Park as the natural and normal entry point into the valley, ironically from Wyoming, not from Colorado. This entry point from Laramie remains the most commonly used entrance today.

In 1878, Jacob Fordyce, who was a friend of James Pinkham, moved his family into North Park. "They were camped near Golden on their way to California" when they had a change of plans.[6] They were the first white family to live in the Park. This was also the time of the early beginnings of the Big Creek Ranch and other ranches, such as the Mendenhall Ranch.

Despite these early efforts of white settlers to move into North Park, the Utes were still present, and the Indians continued to be a threat and a "problem" for the whites; and due to occasional so-called "Indian scares," there would soon be trouble. The trouble, though, did not happen this time in North Park. Instead it happened in Meeker, Colorado.

On September 29, 1879, in what later became known in Colorado history as the "Meeker Massacre," because the victor writes the history, the Utes attacked an Indian Agency in western Colorado killing Nathan Meeker and ten of his male employees, and taking women and children as hostages. This event caused quite a stir among the whites, to put it mildly. There was still active resistance to white intrusions and the efforts to change the Ute's long-held lifestyles. In defense of the Utes, their actions can be seen as a form of protest, as they were resisting Meeker's policies and practices that had forced them to farm and to cease their pony races and hunting forays. Unfortunately, the consequence of this transformative event was the removal of the Northern Ute from Colorado under the authority of the Ute Removal Act passed by the U.S. Congress in 1880.

In the final analysis the Utes were rounded up and placed on the Uintah Reservation in northeastern Utah. This action effectively made millions of acres available in Colorado for settlement by incoming white immigrants, who were eagerly pouring into the area. The "times they were a changing" fast as they sometimes do.

At this point in time in the saga of Walden, it is worthwhile to ponder whether the Native Americans and European whites could have accomplished détente and peaceful co-existence in the State of Colorado. The answer, unfortunately, is probably no. They were different people with different traditions, and more importantly, they had very different lifestyles. The Native Americans were nomadic wanderers, hunters, and gatherers, and the whites were accustomed to establishing permanent settlements and engaging in hunting, ranching, and some mining. This new lifestyle and a different way of living is what Meeker had attempted to instill in the Native Americans, and it had not worked.

So the two groups were on a collision course—and the whites, by their sheer numbers and better technology, prevailed. It is interesting to note and to quote Paul Willard

Richard: "North Park is an exact mini-model of the frontier settlement as it crossed America." Native Americans were displaced and removed from their ancestral lands in almost all states throughout North America. New Mexico is one exception: many Native Americans lived in permanent settlements called "pueblos" and, to a great extent, still live in the ancestral lands they had occupied prior to European contact. The white population, including the Spaniards, were all immigrants that had fled Europe then traveled from other parts of the country and other countries to begin a new life in America.

White pioneer settlers at this time began to move quickly into North Park. On October 20, 1880, Frank Snyder was the first white child born in North Park,[7] and the account of this new birth was recorded for history. The entire population demographics were changing rapidly, and it was all being recorded for posterity.

CHAPTER 4

Mining and the Founding of Walden
(1880 to 1890)

"The future inhabitants of this region, wherever they may place their homes, can be sure that they have been anticipated ... for man is rich in proportion to the things he can let alone."
— Henry David Thoreau

In 1875, there was still serious interest in pursuing mining opportunities in North Park. It was rumored that there was gold, silver, and even copper in those mountains. Some of the evidence for this mining and mineral speculation had come from the aforementioned gold strike on Independence Mountain in 1846, as well as the placer mining taking place at the time, so mining was quite extensive in 1870. On June 10, 1870, there were twenty-four claims staked and as many as 50 miners in North Park.[1]

Teller City was the next mining site in North Park, and it actually grew to become a significant mountain mining hamlet in the southern part of the Park. A post office was established there in 1880, and in 1881, when the town was incorporated, it had a population of about 100. Teller City was named for Colorado Senator Henry M. Teller, and by 1883 the population had grown to 300 and then to 1,300 at its peak.[2] The initial excitement that led to the boom, however, was quickly squashed and was followed by the typical bust, as Teller City collapsed by 1883. "The truth was that the endeavor was mostly a big mining stock fraud."[3] In any case most of the miners left the area, but some stayed and would become homesteaders in North Park.

Marcus Aurelius Walden moved to North Park as a consequence of the mining fever at Teller City. "He first arrived in the Park on a hunting trip with Sam Brownlee in 1879. That same year he came back and filed on a pre-emption claim in Sage Hen Draw fourteen miles southeast of the present site of Walden."[4] As the first postmaster of Walden, he established a post office on his homestead by February 28, 1881.

The Walden post office was then moved to a site near the Cloyd Huston Ranch, on July 23, 1882, with Otto Dunham as postmaster. On October 27, 1883, the third Walden post office was relocated near Sage Hen, southeast of present-day Walden near Highway 14, with Henry H. Richards as postmaster. The fourth Walden post office was established on August 17, 1889, at the present site of Walden, which had up to that point been known as "Points of Rock." The new postmaster was Harriet Peaslee.[5]

Marcus Aurelius Walden, named by his parents for a Roman emperor, was born in 1845 in Virginia. His mother, Lucy Bragg, was the niece of General Bragg, of Confederate and Fort Bragg fame. Walden was fifteen when the Civil War started, and he served during the Civil War presumably as a Confederate soldier.[6] Many early pioneers into North Park served in the Civil War on both the Union and Confederate sides of the conflict.

Walden and his wife, Amelia Jackson Bolteroff, moved to Denver in the late 1860s, after the Civil War ended. He returned to the Park in 1879 with his new wife, Ida George. There's no record of what happened to his first wife. He only lived in North Park for three or four years. He started a post office and ran a guest house, then left North Park for Grand Lake, Colorado, in Middle Park, where he ran a hotel and served as Grand County commissioner for one year. Walden finally departed Colorado for San Francisco, California, where he passed away in 1926, after having lived to the age of eighty-one.[7] Although he never actually lived in the town, Marcus Aurelius Walden is generally considered to be one of the founders of Walden, because he inadvertently became its namesake.

The true founding, or the actual development, of Walden began when civil engineer Ike Greene arrived in 1883. He filed a homestead claim for 160 acres on the Illinois River, where the town of Walden is now located; one year later, he built the town's first house, and Lucien Turner took the claim east of Greene's.[8] Construction on Walden's first public building, the schoolhouse, began by 1885. It was built over five to six years and dedicated in 1891. That same year, Greene built Walden's first church—and even preached in it.

Greene laid out the original townsite using some of his land and some of Turner's. He surveyed the lots for a mere $5 per claim, something that had previously cost $125 to $130, using a surveyor from outside the Park. The lots, 35 x 125 feet, were laid out compactly, like city blocks (270 x 600 feet), with 48 lots in each block. The streets were 60 feet wide and included alleys on the backside. Main Street was 80 feet wide. The streets running from east to west were named First, Second, Third, Fourth, and Fifth streets, and those running north to south were originally A, B, and C streets but were later renamed.[9] This is the reason that Walden, unlike most small rural towns has the feel of having eight compact city blocks out in the country.

Ike Greene donated twenty acres to be used as a community cemetery when his third child, Ivan, died in 1886. Because of all of his good deeds and transformative and consequential initiatives toward the establishment of the town of Walden, Ike Greene should be considered its true founder.

In 1887, Alice Shippey was the first child born in Walden.[10] She married Boon McCallum from another pioneer family and lived in Denver for most of her life.

In 1888, C.E. "Gene" Mosman established C.E. Mosman General Merchandise.[11] It would become the central supply point for the entire Park, and in essence, this made Walden the hub of the Park.

On December 2, 1890, Walden was incorporated as a municipality in the State of Colorado. The population numbered sixty-four. Mosman became the first mayor of Walden through an official action taken by the Walden Town Council on March 2, 1891. In April of 1893, Mosman was elected Mayor of Walden in his own right, with the eleven votes cast by the citizens of Walden.[12]

Gene Mosman should also be considered a legitimate founder of Walden—not just for starting his store or for being the first mayor, as well as holding several important positions—such as postmaster and both town and county treasurer—but also for his diligence as an active and passionate community leader. He served as mayor five different times over more than forty years, the last term being from 1927 to 1932. Mosman passed away in 1931 before completing his final term in office. He was truly a diligent and dedicated public servant, and one of the three substantial founders of the town of Walden.

CHAPTER 5

The Origins of the Cattle Ranching Domain
(Late 1800s)

"I am wont to think that men are not so much the keepers of herds as herds are the keepers of men; the former are so much the freer."
— Henry David Thoreau

After initial forays into hunting and mining, settlers turned to a more dependable enterprise, and cattle ranching became king in North Park. The early attempts at mining were mostly futile with the exception of mining at Pearl, which generated a quick rush of rampant mining fervor in the early 1900s but turned out to be another flash in the pan. The early 1880s saw a "never-ending stream of settlers rushing into North Park, some interested in mining, some interested in ranching."[1] It was the cattle ranchers, though, who established North Park as their domain.

Cattle ranching was the logical, simple, and maybe only viable choice, since the Utes and the bison were gone, and the rich river-bottom meadows were still full of tall, lush grass. Some people, such as Willard Richard, boasted that there was "no better grazing country in the world" than in North Park. Regardless, it would not be easy goings for these hearty and vigilant pioneers to live in North Park permanently for the entire year. Still others have opined that the Indians were the wiser people "because they knew enough to leave" before the long severe winters came roaring in.[2]

In actuality, North Park was not intended to be settled by white Europeans, according to an 1886 Colorado Supreme Court decision that ruled that the territorial legislature of 1861 intended that North Park be part of Larimer County. An excerpt from this decision stated, "Much stress is laid upon the fact that, for a long period of time, Larimer County laid no claim to the territory in dispute. But, in this connection, it must be remembered that the north park is geographically isolated, and, for a long time after the passage of the act organizing the counties of the territory, was uninhabited." According to the testimony, "it was a hunting ground to which it was dangerous for the white man to resort."[3]

Many of the early settlers would leave soon after they arrived. In all likelihood, of those who came to North Park for ranching, more people left than stayed. According to Paul Willard Richard, the winter lasted so long that many would become discouraged and "starve out" or "freeze out."[4] One settler sold his ranch for $50 and left. Another one, Dan McIsaac, "bought the adjoining ranch from a settler, giving him a shotgun and ten dollars for it."[5]

The stalwart, resilient ones who came and persevered built up their ranches and herds, and they succeeded. Without a doubt, Walden would not have been founded without the cattle rancher's presence because it became the central supply point for the ranchers and the entire Park. Walden grew to become the county seat and a successful and vibrant community—indeed, the hub of the Park.[6]

Before the 1879 "Meeker Massacre" and

the 1880 Ute Removal Act, there were no cattle, fences, or ranches in North Park. In the early 1880s, "North Park was little more than an unfenced cattle range."[7] But people like Nick Spicer, visiting the Park from Laramie, would circulate "stories of the beautiful valley full of wild game and a lot of wild hay for feed for the cattle."[8]

It was in 1878, though, that the Big Creek Ranch had its early beginnings in Wyoming.

Just over the state line from North Park, the Big Creek Ranch was started by Jeff and Barney Hunter, and grew to become a huge ranch operation, with up to five thousand to ten thousand cattle in the early years. Two other Hunter brothers, Jack and Tom, also built a ranch that would later become known as the Stateline Ranch.[9] Harry Hunter, nephew of Jeff and Barney Hunter, worked on these ranches and later had an interest in both spreads.

The A Bar A, another big ranch in Wyoming, has become a dude ranch or guest ranch. All three of these ranches were purchased in the 1960s by the Charles C. Gates Sr. family.[10] Another set of ranches that came to be known as the Three Rivers Ranch were owned by Carl Johnson. Another big ranch in North Park was the Big Horn Ranch, which was started by the Hanson family, from Sweden, and then became the Boettcher; later it was owned by A.D. Davis. Still another working ranch, the Swift and Company, became the Two Bar Ranch near Walden.[11] The current Swift Ranch is owned and operated by Bob Swift, whose father was Ralph "Shorty" Swift.

In 1879, the Mendenhall Ranch, which later became the John Payne Ranch, had its start when Montie Blevins and Sam Brownlee drove cattle to North Park because they were in desperate need for cattle feed; the area they were grazing at Virginia Dale, an area between Laramie, Wyoming, and Fort Collins, Colorado, was suffering a severe drought. The Blevins Ranch was also started shortly thereafter, and there would be four generations of Blevinses on the ranch with the name Montie Blevins. Montie Blevins IV was a classmate of the author, F.R. Bob Romero, in the North Park High School graduating class of 1967.

Montie Blevins the first was an accomplished cowboy and cowman, and a notable figure in North Park history. "Due to the man's personal charm and magnetism, everybody liked Montie Blevins."[12] He was born in Iowa in 1859 and "crossed the plains to Colorado in a covered wagon with his parents in 1864. ... At age 14, Montie ran away from home and never returned."[13] In 1877, he went to work for C.B. Mendenhall, at Virginia Dale, then later started his own ranch in North Park.

Small family ranches that were built from scratch, starting with 160-acre homestead claims, would become the norm for North Park. One of these early settlers was Thomas John Payne, a direct immigrant from England who arrived in North Park in 1884. He bought a relinquishment claim north of Cowdrey and built a cattle ranch that grew to be an 800-head Hereford operation. His son Stephen Payne chronicled and paid tribute to the legacy of early-day ranching in the Park with his book, *Where the Rockies Ride Herd* (1965).

Another early ranching family in North

Park was the Jasper (Jap) and Belinda (Lindy) Monroe family, who arrived in the Park in October 1886.[14] They left Custer, Montana, and traveled by wagon in a loop trip through Laramie, Wyoming, and Fort Collins, Colorado, to start a ranch in North Park. A great grandson, Paul Willard Richard, grew up on the Two-Bar Ranch on the northern edge of Walden, and he, too, recorded the story of early-day ranching families in the valley in his book, *Colorado's North Park: History, Wildlife, and Ranching* (2009). Thus, the saga of ranching in North Park has been well documented, but the story of Walden, the hub of the Park, has not.

Beginning in 1880, many of the newcomers in North Park were immigrants and ranchers, and all established connections to Walden. John Henry Brocker was born in Hamburg, Germany, in 1842, and became a naturalized American citizen in Iowa in 1859.[15] He initially came to Colorado to work the mines in Leadville, Blackhawk, and Central City. He was still chasing the glitter of gold dust when he arrived in North Park in 1881. He worked at the End-o-Mile Mine at Teller City,[16] and by the time the mine closed down, he had an interest in it. Brocker took up a homestead, which he developed and ranched. He married Miss Olive Look, and they had three children, one of whom was John Henry Brocker Jr. The younger John Henry stayed in the Park, married Rosa Robertson, and took up a homestead adjoining his folks' near the settlement of Owl.[17]

Ernest Brocker was the elder brother in that family of four children. He married Audrey O'Dell, and they purchased and ran the Bill Simpson Ranch south of Walden in the late 1950s. Their children, Rosa Mae and Gordon, grew up on the family ranch as fourth-generation North Parkers. In the early 1960s, at least three of the author's cousins from Taos, New Mexico, worked on the Brocker Ranch during hay season. The ranch was sold to the U.S. government in 1965 and became part of the Arapaho National Wildlife refuge—or the "Duck Farm," as it is called by locals.

George and Rosalie Allard came to North Park from Canada around 1886.[18] They had followed her father, James Pinkham, the proprietor of the roadhouse at Pinkhampton, and ran the roadhouse for a number of years. In chain-migration style, a good number of Allards immigrated to the Park; but over time, some of them returned to Canada. The Allards married into other pioneer families and developed cattle ranches. The majority of those who settled in North Park either descended from immigrants or were immigrants themselves.

James and Joe Murphy were born on Prince Edward Island, Canada. They came to Leadville in 1880 and built homes, but later discovered that the title to their land was no good. So the brothers moved almost due north (as the crow flies) to North Park, in 1884, and took up cattle ranching. Joe homesteaded on Grizzly Creek and ran a small herd of Shorthorn cattle and later some Herefords. He married Margaret Doyle, and they had two sons, Earl and Francis. Earl passed away in 1908 and Francis (known as Pat) worked the ranch with his father. Upon his father's death, he assumed full responsibility for the management of the ranch.[19]

Pat married Bertha Langholf, and the couple moved to the town of Walden in 1956. He was active in many organizations, including the Mountain Parks Electric REA, North Park Stock Growers Association, and the Bureau of Land Management (BLM) advisory committee. They were wonderful people, and the author delivered the *Rocky Mountain News* to them in the late 1950s and 1960s, secretly wishing the elderly couple would adopt him so he could live on a cattle ranch.

Many North Park families immigrated directly from Sweden. William and Andrew Norell came to Colorado in 1882 to start cattle ranching.[20] They started a chain migration of Swedes that included Victor Hanson; Carl D. Johnson; Andrew, John, and Elias Peterson; Carl Erickson; F.G. Gus Carlstrom; and Carl Carlstrom. All of these families developed ranches in North Park.

Marion Carlstrom Trick was born on the Lone Pine Ranch, but her father Carl Carlstrom later purchased the Harmon Ranch near Cowdrey in 1928 and operated it into his eighties.[21] When he passed, the ranch became the Carl and Marion Carlstrom Trick Ranch. Clarence Romero, brother to the author, worked in the hay fields at this ranch every summer during his high school days with his good friend and classmate Carl Trick Jr. There was a symbiotic and friendly relationship between the kids who lived on the ranch and the kids who lived in town. Ranching families were thought of as royalty within the schools and the community.

While in high school, the author and an older brother, Joe, worked at the Meyring Livestock Company owned by Oliver "Twist" Meyring and Ruth Coyte Meyring and their families.[22] Ruth descended from Ralph Coyte, who was an early-day pioneer in North Park. Twist arrived in North Park in the 1920s and married Ruth. Their sons were Jerry, David, and Dan. In 1965, Dan taught the author the intricacies of scatter raking, such as how to move a twenty-one-foot scatter rake through a fourteen-foot gate. Dan explained and demonstrated the process in a very matter-of-fact way. "You drive forward and wrap the left side of the rake around the left gate post, as you ease the right side of the rake past the right gate post. You then back up, turn the steering wheel sharply to the right, and you move forward into the next field." This little trick of the trade was essential for the person on the haying crew who was operating the scatter rake to move swiftly from field to field.

Besides the tasty food in the bunkhouse kitchen and in the field, another memorable experience was to see the stacking crew in action with horse-drawn sweeps that would deliver a load of hay to the haystack. Twist Meyring would then use his homemade horse-operated pusher to push the hay up the slide stacker and into the haystack. Jack Greene, son of Ike Greene, invented the slide stacker in 1897. Another North Parker, Joe Lawrence, invented the pusher.[23] The author also worked at the tail end of one haying season at the Jack Dickens Ranch on the east side of the Park.

Haying was an essential task for managing and maintaining a cattle ranch. Besides the ranching family, a summer haying crew might include such a diverse group as Louie La Plant, an Indian from New Mexico;

Don Clark, from Chicago; Jose Paloma, a washed-up boxer from Texas; several "winos" (as they were referred to) from Larimer Street in Denver, and lots of teenagers. The hay had to be put up with whatever labor force the ranching families could cobble together, because the cows had to be fed for the entire long winter.

The early pioneers learned this hard lesson when they first attempted to let cows forage on the open range. In the deadly winter of 1883-84, some lost nearly half their stock.[24] Similarly, in the winter of 1898-99, it was reinforced that if you wanted to run cattle in North Park, you had to put up hay in the summer to feed in the winter. "Make hay while the sun shines" was the common refrain heard on the ranches. Some ranchers, like Lindy Monroe, would say that "North Park has nine months of winter and three months late in the fall."[25] For most ranchers like the Paynes, though, the routine and the seasons were before haying, haying, after haying, and winter.[26] For families living in Walden, it was more like nine months of winter and three months of mosquitos.

There were numerous family ranchers in North Park—too many to name them all. They included the Manvilles, Brownlees, Humberts, Foxes, Hamptons, Riggens, Dodges, Van Valkenbergs, Wattenbergs, and others who provided seasonal employment for Walden's teenagers. Ranch work included dragging the meadows and branding the cows in the spring. On branding day, the author would round up a friend or two in town, like Jerry Follett, and they would go out and wrestle the new calves that had to be branded, vaccinated, dehorned and doctored. These Walden teenagers would collect the euphemistically named "Rocky Mountain oysters" in a jar and fry them later at home.

North Park ranchers generally considered themselves to be cowboys, or stockmen who ran cattle. Only a few ranchers—like Elmer Mallon, George Baily, Ernest Brocker, and Jasper Monroe—attempted to introduce sheep.[27] When they did, sheepherders from northern New Mexico, where sheep had been dominant for four hundred years, would travel to Colorado or other

Rocky Mountain states to herd them.[28] But the raising of sheep caused concern among some of the cattlemen, and the practice was not that well received in cattle country, so cattle remained dominant in North Park.[29]

The summer rodeo, which was renamed the "Never Summer Rodeo," was popular in Walden, and steer roping was an event that North Park ranchers were attracted to enjoyed. There were some ranchers though, like Jasper Monroe, who did not view most rodeo events as relevant to actual ranch work, skills, and practices. For example, no one would actually jump off a horse and wrestle a steer to the ground or ride a "twisting and bucking bull," or even rope a calf running at full speed.[30] Nonetheless, the ranchers and community of Walden participated in the sport wholeheartedly.

It is interesting to ponder whether or not many of the North Park stockmen and cowboys were fully aware of the true origins of most of the ranching skills, language, and terms used around the cowboy lifestyle. "It was the Spanish who first brought modern horses—and domesticated cattle—to America in the 16th century, and the influence of their culture and traditions is apparent in everyday conversation on ranches today."[31]

The term cowboy is a direct translation of the term vaquero which was popular in the Southwest in the 1800s; the word later became "buckaroo" to the Western cowboy. The term rodeo came from the Spanish word rodear, to "round up" the cattle. Many of the terms used for equipment and clothing were derived from the Spanish language: chaps from chapas and lariat from larieta. To "dally," or to wrap the rope around the saddle horn, came from the common retort in Spanish dale vuelta. A rope made from horsehair was called a McCarty. "The word came from the Spanish Mescate and has been Americanized to McCarty."[32] So in essence, many of the words used on the ranch, including names for horses such as palomino, pinto, and mustang (mesteño) came from the vaquero of the Southwest.

For the early cowmen, and even the later-day ranch families, solitude was an ever-present companion, especially in the winter. Like Henry David Thoreau at Massachusetts' Walden Pond, they learned to love—or at least to accept—their solitude. Stephen Payne described it as "the relentless winter, the sameness of our meals, and the job which became a monotonous grind …"[33] The quietness was so great that many were ready to leave Colorado's "Walden Pond" soon after they had arrived. But the resilient families persevered. The older generation had to remain vigilant until the next generation could assume the responsibility of managing the ranch. Many of the ranch families owned houses in Walden, and some would eventually retire to live in town.

Routine ranching tasks were demanding. Meadows had to be fertilized and irrigated, fences had to be built and maintained, cattle had to be branded and doctored, herded and fed, and enough hay had to be baled and put up to sustain the cattle throughout the winter. As noted by Paul Willard Richard, ranchers were "owned by their hay, their cattle, and their ranch land, and they scurried about to serve them in an almost self-containing cycle."[34] Essentially, they were tied down by their cattle, and not so much the reverse. As Henry David Thoreau put it, "... men are not so much the keepers of herds as herds are the keepers of men; the former are so much the freer."[35]

The future of ranching in North Park is uncertain and unpredictable. Ranches are increasingly owned by corporations or absent wealthy owners, and family ranching is a shrinking activity.[36] In Richards' words, "North Parkers should hope for the best, expect the worst, and be prepared for the impossible.[37] One might add that they should envision and embrace what is possible.

CHAPTER 6

Early Twentieth Century in Walden
(1900 to 1920)

"Will you be a reader, a student merely, or a seer? Read your fate, see what is before you and walk on into futurity."
— HENRY DAVID THOREAU

By the turn of the century, Walden's population had grown to 141. Over the next twenty years, the events and activities that unfolded there would have a lasting impact for the rest of the twentieth century. Waldenites, as Thoreau suggested, would read their fate, see what was before them, and walk into the future.

On September 14, 1895, the Town of Walden trustees awarded a contract for construction of a jail, which was apparently the second public building owned by the town. In 1896, the first Walden Town Hall was constructed. Prior to this, most public meetings took place either at the schoolhouse, the first public building in Walden, or at the Mosman Store, which later evolved into something of a community center, called Mosman Hall. That same year, the Town donated $25 to help in the construction of the community Methodist church. Walden's first church had been built by Ike Greene in 1891.[1]

Francis E. Milner arrived in Steamboat Springs, Colorado, in 1880, and moved to Walden around 1901. Milner established and became president of the North Park Bank, Walden's first.[2] Initially housed at the brand-new International Order of Oddfellows (I.O.O.F.) building on Main Street, by 1911 it had been moved to a building owned by the bank.[3] The townspeople were not necessarily expecting to get rich by having a bank in town, but they were hoping to see more personal wealth contributing to a more prospering community.

In 1892, Walden waterworks consisted of a windmill and a well. On October 27, 1894, town trustees purchased a 100-barrel water tank and water rights from the Riggen Ditch. In 1904, the first true waterworks system was initiated when they voted to secure 100 acre feet of water from the Riggen Ditch and issued $14,000 in water bonds to fund the public water system and more efficiently supply water to the town of Walden.[4] The town's first firehouse was also built in 1904, by E.F. Loffer, for $60.[5] The public sewer system would not be constructed until the 1950s, and other public-works projects—such as paved streets, curbs, and sidewalks—would eventually be installed.

Then in 1905, the Telephone Exchange brought telephone service to Walden and North Park.[6] Some of the phone lines were even placed along and on top of barbed-wire fences that by then were common in the Park. In 1905, the Park Range Forest Reserve became the Routt National Forest, and a more stringent practice regarding the management of public lands would ensue from that point forward.

On September 5, 1907, a fire company was organized.[7] The Walden Volunteer Fire Department was not organized until 1939, but it continues to serve the area to this day.

The first automobiles in Walden created quite a commotion.[8] As reported in the September 5, 1907, edition of the New Era newspaper, "The wild eyed expressions of our towns people and the nervous prostrations suffered by the horses in the Park, are due to the advent into Walden of some five or six automobiles."[9] Stephen Payne related in his book that almost everyone still maintained that, "Them horseless buggies'll never be practical."[10]

The efforts to establish Jackson County were difficult and contentious. Many people felt that a new county was needed because Fort Collins, the county seat of Larimer County, was far away and extremely difficult to get to when county transactions were required, especially in the winter.[11] Some were against it because they could not afford additional taxes. At least one argument between the Swede Andrew Norell and Charlie Baker, who was circulating a petition for the new county, transpired. Baker snorted, "You blankety-blank foreigners believe you can come over to our country ...

but I'm telling you..." "Foreigner yourself!" Norell exploded. "You come from Missouri and dot ain't in the United States."[12] The area had initially been part of Grand County and then was made up of parts of two counties—mostly Larimer with a small section of Grand. The ranchers tended to be against forming a county, but with the objective in the works for a while, many people, especially those living in Walden, were in favor.

K.J. (Kenneth) MacCallum was a central figure in the effort to create Jackson County. A North Park horseman since the early1880s, he worked and owned horses at the Boettcher Ranch and also traveled far and wide outside the area. On one of his trips outside the Park in 1889, he bet on the wrong horse at the Kentucky Derby (Proctor Knott) and lost most of his money. He returned to North Park and went to work at the C.E. Mosman Merchandise Store. He also worked as a cashier and later became vice president then president at North Park Bank. McCallum was a member of the town council and served as Walden's mayor from

1899 to 1900 and again from 1912 to 1916. He also served for five years as the county judge, from 1927 to 1931.[13]

K.J. MacCallum had a strong connection to Larimer County. At one point he banked at the Poudre Valley Bank in Fort Collins and served as deputy sheriff of Larimer County, with his headquarters in Walden.[14] He was elected as a Larimer County Commissioner and was strategically positioned when, as chairman, he called to order a special meeting of the Larimer County Commission on June 3, 1909. It had been decreed in May 1909 by the General Assembly of the State of Colorado that a county be formed and the boundary lines be determined.[15]

The first item on the Commission's agenda was the resolution for the birth of Jackson County. Others at the meeting were the already appointed Jackson County Commissioners Hugh Hunter, J.E. Elmer Mallon, and Owen C. Case. The resolution passed and Jackson County was born, with Walden as the county seat. In essence, Jackson County was the creation of the Town of Walden. The town trustees donated $250, and it all happened with the help of others who were involved with town government, especially K.J. MacCallum.[17] The establishment of Jackson County, named after President Andrew Jackson, ushered in an economic and building boom in Walden. The population of Jackson County grew to 1,013 in the 1910 census, with 162 people living in Walden.

In the division of county funds and the settlement of assets, Jackson County received a fund balance of $3,633.82: $2,530.41 for its share of school funds, one wagon, one pick, and two shovels. In addition to the three other county commissioners, the following were the first officers of Jackson County: B.C. Boston, sheriff; E.N. "Ernest" Butler, clerk and recorder; W.O. Mosman, treasurer; S.E. Swire, assessor; J.T. Shippey, county judge; Mrs. Eva Dawson, superintendent of schools; and A.G. Maine, coroner.[16]

The arrival of the railroad presented a vision for a new era of prosperity.[17] Some called it "the greatest event in the history of North Park,"[18] and it had taken "more than 25 years for the event to be realized." The Laramie Plains Line was built to transport goods in and out of the county. As declared in speeches on Railroad Day, on October 25, 1911, "We now have transportation facilities, the one thing we lacked to make it [Jackson] one of the best counties of Colorado. We have an unlimited amount of fine coal, besides silver, gold, lead, copper, and zinc. We raise the finest hay, barley, rye, oats, wheat, and vegetables. Our cattle are noted all over the United States ... the coming of a larger population from the east to our county which will settle up the vacant land and make our barren places to bloom like a garden." Some of it was hyperbole, but the railroad line built from Laramie—the Hahn's Peak and Pacific Line, also known as the Laramie Plains Line or the "long hard pull"—came to fruition with great expectations and hopes for growth and an era of prosperity in Walden and Jackson County.[19]

The august county courthouse, perhaps the most impressive and stately building in Walden, was planned and designed by architect William C. Bowman in 1912, and built by contractor J.H. Searles in 1913.[20] It was constructed using sandstone from a hill north of Walden and native limestone from a quarry on the Mendenhall Ranch.[21] Conflicting sources put the cost between $28,000 and $40,000. The same commissioners who had served since the inception of the county were involved, and two new commissioners, Malcolm C. Ward and Harry Green, were there when the building was erected.[22] Archie Hunter later donated the land on which the courthouse now stands at the center of Fourth Street. Six lots surrounding the building were "purchased from E.J. Norris to square the lot."[23] The North Park Pioneer Museum was developed and dedicated on the west side of the property in the 1960s.

In 1913, Art Wilkens founded the *Jackson County Star*.[24] A number of newspapers had been started and had circulated in Walden and North Park, including *The Prospector, The North Park Miner, The Grand County Times, North Park Union, Pearl Mining Times, Jackson County Times, New Era*, and *North Park News*. Wilkens bought the *New Era* from Carl McFadden and merged it with his newspaper. The *Jackson County Star* celebrated its 100-

year anniversary in 2013 and has proved its diligence. The newspaper passed the test of time with a number of editors, and its longevity makes the *Jackson County Star* one of the fixtures of permanence in Walden.

In 1910, a strange incident occurred in Walden related to the town's public water system and the editor of the *New Era* newspaper. It was reported in the May 6, 1910, edition of *The Grand Encampment Herald* to have transpired as follows:

> "Alfred Law, a lawyer and editor of the New Era newspaper in Walden, Co. was shot through the right lung by J.N. Davis, an employee of W.O. Mosman. Mr. Davis wanted a retraction of a story by Mr. Law that suggested Mr. Davis was responsible for the town of Walden going dry. Mr. Davis had been employed as the engineer at the city water plant. He was replaced by A.N. Siebert. Soon afterward, Siebert had trouble getting water into the stand pipe, and it was discovered that the valve had been tampered with. Law published a statement saying

that if Davis had not tampered with the valve then his friends had made it look suspicious for him. After shooting Law, Mr. Davis asked, "Did I get him?" and went into the Mosman's store and shot himself in the head. He died four hours later. The fate of Mr. Law was unknown at the time of the printing."[25]

This is an example of a historical event that is only a footnote in history but that occasionally happens in every community—usually surrounding individual characters, the local media, and a town's public waterworks or local government—when the truth is stranger than fiction. But for all its weirdness, it is still part of the town's history.

A three-phase generator, brought in by Walter Lyerman in 1916, became the first public light plant in Walden. The first commercial light plant was started by Hartford Loucks in 1918, but widespread electric power for the majority of people in Walden would not be available until 1950, when the Mountain Parks Electric rural electric association (REA) was started. It is interesting to note that Walden apparently had telephone service before it had electricity. Starting with Carter Oil, which began drilling in North Park in 1920, natural gas and oil as an energy source became available in Walden.

At this point in time, starting in the 1920s, Walden was beginning to see the development of prosperous new industries, with associated employment opportunities, and it was moving swiftly into the twentieth century and into its "futurity."

CHAPTER 7

The Employment/Industries: Government, Education, Mining, Timber, Gas and Oil, Railroad, Retail, Outdoor Recreation, and Tourism
(1920s to late 1900s)

"In short, I am convinced, both by faith and experience, that to maintain one's self on this earth is not a hardship but a pastime, if we will live simply and wisely."
— HENRY DAVID THOREAU

Throughout the twentieth century, employment opportunities in various old and new industries became available in Walden, helping to create a diversified economy. Cattle ranching remained king in the county, but gainful employment could be had in government, education, mining, timber, gas and oil, railroad, outdoor recreation, and some tourism.

Most people even during the 1930s depression were able to maintain and provide for themselves and their families, and they did.

Some people were able to work for local government, either for the Town of Walden or Jackson County, or even for the federal government, in jobs for such agencies as the Forest Service. The Mountain Parks Electric REA provided jobs to build and maintain the electric grid.

The public schools offered jobs for teachers, administrators, coaches, cafeteria workers, and janitors. The schoolhouse was one of the first buildings constructed in Walden. The people streaming into North Park in the 1880s-'90s were a literate bunch: They published newspapers and made schools and educational opportunity a priority. The school system grew from a one-classroom county-operated schoolhouse with few students into a district-operated school with a superintendent and elected school board. By 1944, 210 students were enrolled in Walden's schools, and by the middle of the twentieth century, the Jackson County School District had 400 students and more than fifteen teachers.[1]

The Walden school system was a credible rural district, with good teachers throughout the system. A student enrolled in Walden schools in the 1960s (North Park School District R-1) was sure to have at least one outstanding teacher at each level. There were no huge government-mandated programs or an emphasis on mass testing or standards, or clichés such as No Child Left Behind, but the system educated the children adequately and prepared them for jobs and for life.

Historically, mining in North Park had its booms and busts. Early on, some people touted gold, silver, and copper mining, but in reality not much of any of these minerals was mined or found in Jackson County. Coal, however, which as far back as 1886 had not been heard of in North Park, especially low-sulfur coal, was found in abundance at Coalmont. The colloquially called "coal holes" from which North Parkers collected their winter coal were claimed and surveyed by the Union Pacific Railroad.[2]

The Riach Brothers filed a claim and began to develop a mine and built the town of Coalmont. The railroad was built to

Coalmont to facilitate shipping. "Coal mining was a very important industry for North Park for many years and much was shipped to outside points." Coal was widely used in the Park for the schoolhouse and anywhere people congregated. "In 1929 there were about 60 dwelling houses in Coalmont, in addition to the store, post office, warehouse, bath house-office, stables, etc., with a school house in the center of the community. Population was about 200," only slightly less than Walden at the time.[3]

At some point in time a "serious fire broke out in the mine at Coalmont."[4] The fire was contained temporarily, but eventually the mine had to be abandoned. For decades, smoke could be seen rising out the ground in the vicinity of the mine. The Rosebud Coal Company built and operated a crusher and strip-mined coal there in the early 1960s. But by 1970, the coal mine was no longer in operation, and nothing but a post office was left in Coalmont.

Other coal-mining ventures were present during the twentieth century, particularly on the east side of the Park, but they generally proved successful for only short periods of time. One of the last to shut down operations, the A.D. Kerr Coal Company, closed its gates in 1981.

Fluorspar, or fluorite, was another mineral that had been mined in North Park since the 1920s; 18,000 tons had been shipped out by 1926, and the total fluorspar from the Northgate district, through 1945, amounted to approximately 45,500 tons. A major mining operation near Northgate was managed by Colorado Fluorspar Corporation in the 1940s and '50s. Ozark-Mahoning continued to mine fluorite and ship it out on the railroad from 1968 to 1974. "Fluorspar turned out to be the most important ore discovery in North Park,"[5] and the Walden student population peaked during that time. The mine's closing down had a negative economic impact on Walden. The student population, which had peaked during the fluorspar era, dwindled. Rex Shaw served as caretaker of the mine from 1976 to 1986.[6]

The oil-and-gas industry in North Park has also had its peaks and valleys, but it did provide some jobs. Continental Oil

Company established its North Park presence in the early 1920s. "Continental Oil's famous ice-cream well was named for the frost created on pipes and machinery by the carbon dioxide in it blew in on December 16, 1926."[7] By 1960, the North Callum Oil Field was annually producing $2.5 million worth of oil. Various independent wildcat oil operations sprouted up periodically throughout the Park before the wells were virtually pumped dry. Currently, some new wells continue to pump oil with current technologies in what has become a twenty-first-century oil boom in North Park. The last of the producing natural-gas wells dried up in 1994, but with the new technology, some have recently come back online. The gas utility that provides natural gas in Walden is owned by the Town of Walden.

The timber industry was a lucrative windfall for many people living in North Park. In the early 1900s, a number of small sawmills were in operation in the Park by individuals like Bob Pardew, who came to North Park in 1903.[8] In 1936, a U.S. government national timber sale took place in Gould, Colorado, twenty-seven miles southeast of Walden.[9] Michigan River Timber Company (MRTC) built a large sawmill in Walden, where the lumber was sawed, milled, graded, stacked, and shipped. The MRTC operated the sawmill for years, providing countless jobs for people living in Walden. Other operations, such Langendorf Inc., also operated a sawmill in town. Timber camps, such as the Bockman Lumber Camp, popped up in the forest with slab-sided homes for workers. At that time, "industrial development of lumber in North Park ranked second only to the cattle industry."[10] People were employed at the sawmills in Walden, as lumberjacks and skidders in the woods, and as independent truckers hauling logs from the forest to the sawmills. By the late 1940s, the chainsaw became available, making timbering much easier for workers and more profitable for the sawmill owners. The population of Gould reached 300 by 1949.[11]

In 1950 another national timber sale took place in Rand, Colorado, and MRTC continued operations at the Walden sawmill with logs trucked in from Rand. The population of Gould nosedived to about fifty residents by 1953, when timbering moved to Rand.[12]

Jobs became available during this time "for people from other parts of the country" who were looking for work.[13] Many arrived from Missouri to work in the woods, which is interesting because several of the people who had arrived in North Park in the late 1800s were also from Missouri and Arkansas. This new injection of people had a distinct influence on the cultural characteristics of North Park. In addition to a Western "cowboy" accent, the North Park twang also developed the noticeable inflection of a Missourian.

"The introduction of sawmills resulted in a significant increase in the population of Walden that impacted its growth and economy for many years."[14] By 1960 the town's population reached 609. Especially for those living in town, the timber industry was the mainstay for employment until 1994, when the sawmill, then under the management of Louisiana Pacific, closed shop.[15]

A passionate debate continues to this day as to whether the closure was due to political pressure from environmentalists, who wanted to stop logging on federal lands, or simply the economic reality that the best locations were logged out. Economically, it was more feasible to timber in other locations around the country, where it takes about ten years to grow the desired tall trees rather than the 125 years it takes in North Park.[16] As was the case with the fate of the Native Americans who were hunting the grazing bison, nothing lasts forever, and the industrial timber industry moved on.

The railroad, when it arrived in Walden in 1911, provided good jobs throughout the twentieth century. Many locals also benefited from the availability of transportation for goods produced in North Park. Families such as the Romeros, Mondragons, and Sanchezes—and even Greek immigrants, like Sam Poulas—came to Walden and were employed by the Union Pacific Railroad (UPRR). The Romero family and others from Northern New Mexico, where few good jobs existed, arrived as "economic refugees" to work on the railroad and worked there until retirement. With the closure of the sawmills and mines, however, the UPRR began the process of leaving Walden between 1994 and 1997.

Commercial retail jobs were also available at places such as the Texaco, Standard, or Conoco gas stations; Timberline and Ken's Builder Supply; restaurants such as the Walden Cafe and the Elkhorn Cafe; grocery stores such as Fair Share, Corkle's Little Market, and Mini-Mart; and so on. Mechanics, carpenters, plumbers, electricians, or other skilled workers were able to find employment. Outdoor recreation such as fishing hunting and snowmobiling, which became popular with North Parkers in the 1960s, continues to provide employment to a few.

Tourism has not attained a good foothold in the area, but it may yet become the most feasible industry for the area. North Park's history, natural environment, and wildlife are interesting and spectacular, posing some hope and potential for Walden that will be explored further in the next chapter. As Henry David Thoreau stated, though, "To maintain one's self on this earth is not a hardship but a pastime, if we will live simply and wisely" and, one could add, frugally. This is especially true in a time of climate change and pandemics, when it may become imperative to disperse populations from the cities and suburban areas and relocate them in rural places like Walden.

CHAPTER 8

The Future of Walden: Assumptions, New Trends, and Potential

"If a man does not keep pace with his companions, perhaps it is because he hears a different drummer. Let him step to the music which he hears, however measured or far away."
— HENRY DAVID THOREAU

Walden has been losing industries, jobs, and population for the past forty years. In 1980, its population peaked at 947, as did the population of Jackson County, at 1,863. The 2020 census puts Walden's population at 500 and Jackson County's at 1,300. During this same time, Colorado's population more than doubled. Several of Walden's major employers shut down operations in that period: Ozark Mahoning in 1974, Kerr Coal in 1981, and both Louisiana Pacific and the Union Pacific railroads in the 1990s. The trends are undeniable, and the truth is that Walden did not keep pace. The pertinent question now is, what is the future of Walden? Considering emerging national and global trends, the author suggests that the future could be bright.

Some assumptions can be made about Walden's future. The town had a diversified economy in the past and could realize this objective again. Ideally, communities strive for a diverse economy with at least one major industry. Throughout its history, Walden has attracted a variety of industries that have impacted its economy, and that have even thrived temporarily. They include ranching, government, mining, timbering, gas and oil, and outdoor recreation, as discussed in previous chapters. The problem has been that most of these industries have not been reliable or sustainable for long periods of time. In addition, most of them have failed to provide large numbers of employees with high salaries or wages. This reality is not unique to Walden. It is a dilemma currently facing most rural communities, especially those that have been based historically on agriculture.

Emerging trends are favorable for the revitalization of small, rural communities. In the United States, the flight from rural communities to large cities has been an ongoing phenomenon for about a century. People move to urban areas for various reasons: Cities are where the jobs are, especially better-paying jobs. A city provides amenities that are not available in rural communities. Shopping malls; restaurants; cultural institutions; airports; medical care and hospitals; higher education; entertainment; and creative, intellectual, and social opportunities have all lured many from rural areas.

These perceived benefits are no longer exclusive to cities. Society has changed dramatically since the advent and availability of the internet in the 1990s. Social media, wireless internet, artificial intelligence, virtual meetings, education, telehealth, and telecommuting are all growing trends.

As long as there is a reliable internet connection, people can be engaged and work from anywhere in the world, even accessing higher education through remote learning in public and private schools and institutions. The problem confronting Walden, and all rural areas, is the ongoing issue of equitable broadband access.[1]

If broadband service can be improved, people living in or visiting Walden will have less need to be in the city. They can work online and get most of what they need on the internet and thus do not have to navigate the busy interstate highways every day. People, though, especially the younger generations, may not yet be ready to give up on life in the city, despite its ever-present congestion, pollution, traffic, crime, and high cost of living.

This book is being written in the middle of the 2020-21 Covid-19 pandemic. The greatest concern is everyday contact with others. The need for social distancing has created a major problem, and many have relocated away from high-population centers since the pandemic began. Realtors acknowledge and are seeing this new trend on the ground, of people proactively taking measures to move out of the cities and back to smaller communities. This is probably going to continue, albeit at a gradual pace.

Climate change, a topic of discussion and debate for some time, is another factor working against the hyper-urbanization of the past century. Scientists are warning that coastal cities like Miami and New Orleans are beginning to see the negative effects of global warming, such as severe weather, and will experience rising water levels within two to three decades—or sooner. As a result, some cities may not be as habitable as they are now, and consequently there could be a significant migration back to the interior of the country.

The rise of mega- or even modest-sized cities was not what Thomas Jefferson envisioned for the United States. Neither did he likely imagine the large number of small towns that are shrinking and dying. Jefferson's vision was one of people living on small farms and providing for themselves and their neighbors. The Jeffersonian view is probably no longer viable, but it may be possible to save small towns if people return to the countryside, working from home on the internet and engaging in small-scale subsistence agriculture and organic farming.

People living in New Mexico since the early 1700s had a vibrant subsistence agrarian society for several centuries that did not depend on the market, and it lasted until about 1950.[2] While the agrarian lifestyle may not be possible or even desirable for all communities, New Mexico offers another option and further proof that it can exist, and it's right in line with Thoreau's advice on how we should live.

In addition, people would have to learn to appreciate the benefits of rural life. Online college courses are available on this topic at schools such as New Mexico Highlands University. The author personally prefers the rural setting and lifestyle that offers outdoor recreation that includes fishing, hunting, hiking, camping, horseback riding, snowmobiling, biking, skiing, and rafting. When you live in the country, you do not have to deal with the issues and stress associated with the city. You have more personal time to be home with family, pets, and livestock. And more time for your pastimes and hobbies.

To appreciate the rural lifestyle and the isolation and solitude it entails is one thing. Some people do, but for others it is difficult. Early pioneers in North Park had no choice but to adapt to their quiet surroundings and the solitude, especially during the long winter months. Henry David Thoreau at Walden Pond learned to love his solitude while living in nature.

Walden, Colorado, has survived for 130 years, and one reason is its location. Situated in the center of North Park, Walden is the community most easily accessible to everyone living in the Park. Other early-day communities had their heyday but either did not grow or did not sustain their original enthusiasm. Teller City and Pearl had their booms and busts but became ghost towns. In 1901, John L. Hilton did all he could to promote Cowdrey and provoke a boom there when he advertised the following in the *North Park Union* newspaper: "Corner lots will be sold for $75.00 while inside lots will be sold for $50.00 each."[3] Despite his efforts and the fact that it was somewhat centrally located, Cowdrey never grew.

Coalmont had its day in the sun, with coal mining and a population that grew to 200 in 1929. But for various reasons, the operations were shut down over time. Gould had a timber boom in 1936, and the population grew to 300 by 1949, until another timber sale moved the jobs to Rand. Walden, however, had steady growth from its incorporation in 1890 until 1980. During the 1950s and '60s, when the author was growing up there, Walden was a vibrant community with excellent schools, some good jobs in the public and private sectors, profitable businesses, and dependable government services.

Perhaps the best game plan for the future of Walden is to continue to encourage the revival of old industries (such as oil and gas) and timber operations (such as the Pellet Mill), while promoting and marketing Walden as an idyllic place for city folks to visit or move to. Target populations could be retirees or people who are financially secure. This might include previous Walden residents who would like to return.

Other demographics to target could be tech-savvy young people looking for adventure and outdoor recreation. As recommended in the 2012 Walden Master Plan, biking, hiking, and snowmobile trails could be developed to link Walden Reservoir, Walden Wetlands, the sand hills, and the Arapaho Wildlife Refuge. The sand hills could be featured as a laid-back recreational area complete with an RV park for extended stays. This adventure tourism initiative would need to be coordinated between local, state, and federal governments, as different jurisdictions are affected. The Wildlife Refuge could be highlighted for animal lovers, and Walden could keep its slogan as the "Moose Viewing Capital of Colorado." Advertising and social digital media marketing could be utilized to promote Walden and the surrounding area as "Colorado's Walden Pond."

Like the A Bar A Ranch, other cattle ranches could be promoted as dude, guest, or working ranches, where visitors could experience life on a ranch that includes haying, branding, and horseback riding. Some ranches will continue operations as working ranches, whether they are family or corporate owned. In addition to converting their ranches to better serve backpackers, hunters, and other outdoor enthusiasts, "Many ranch people are leasing their fishing waters, taking in sportsmen, and providing sites and lodging for snowmobile riders, dirt bikers, ATV'ers and ski headquarters, as well as converting ranches to better serve backpackers, hunters, and outdoor visitors."[4]

"Ranching is no longer the only king in the valley. Thus, nature is slowly coming full cycle in the Park."[5] We could now be seeing a return to Thoreau's idea of "back to nature" or, as suggested by the title of this book, "Back to Walden." One could envision a return to the way things were when new adventurers and tourists were coming to North Park in the 1800s.

Walden has a low crime rate, good local and county government, and solid infrastructure, which must be continually improved, maintained, renovated, and upgraded in accordance with an Infrastructure

Master Plan. Hanson Park could be enhanced to make it more attractive to visitors and residents alike. An enhanced medical facility and pharmacy are needed; Walden had these services before and can realize them again.

A higher-education program would contribute to the community's viability. Perhaps, thinking out of the box, a branch college campus of Walden University should be considered and pursued. Walden University is the most successful fully accredited online university in the country. From a practical and logistical standpoint, all that would be needed is an educational center or office with an internet connection and a coordinator to promote the program.

Tourism in general is a clean industry that has potential in Walden. Walden is an intriguing place with a typical history as a small rural town. It follows the path and model of many communities, with its own uniqueness and idiosyncrasies. The geography is beautiful and pristine. Winters are a challenge, but if a person has the tenacity and perseverance to survive one winter in

Walden, they can survive anything they encounter in life. Bed-and-breakfast sites and vacation rentals could promote their business by advertising package offers to spend a winter in Walden at a discount rate. Indoor and outdoor activities could be organized by the Chamber of Commerce, North Park Heart and Soul, and other tourism advocates. Even the idea of attracting part-time summer residents, as the Indians were attracted in summer, could be promoted.

In any case, the spirit of Walden is alive and well, whether in the spirit of the Native American bison hunters who survived there for 400 years or the spirit of the early European pioneers, be they explorers, mountain men, miners, ranchers, or later-day lumberjacks, railroad section hands, teachers, nurses, linemen, roughnecks, bankers, or entrepreneurs.

In summary, Walden has potential and will survive. It has existed for 130-plus years. The citizens of Walden are survivors; they are strong, active, and engaged. They are also resilient, practical, and tenacious, and they will persevere. Some Waldenites are happy to keep Walden as it is. In concert with Thoreau, if a man hears a different drummer, "let him step to the music which he hears, however measured or far away."

Afterword

Henry David Thoreau's classic *Walden* is about getting back to nature and life in the woods or in the country. It is a reflection upon simple living in natural surroundings. In a sense it is a manual for self-reliance, living simply and frugally. *Walden* is a literary masterpiece that I encountered early in my college career in an American literature class, and it made a big impression on my philosophy of life.

The fact that I had grown up in Walden, Colorado, made me wonder about the synchronicity of the nature theme and the Walden theme, and their influence on me. Then when my daughter graduated from Walden University in 2019 with a PhD in education, I knew that writing this book was autotelic. It just had to be done, as was suggested to me by my editor.

Thoreau believed that "wisdom came from nature." In his two years at Walden

Pond he "attempted to cut himself off from the dictates of society."[1] "In some ways, Walden can be read as a lament for a disappearing America, as a predominantly rural, agricultural life that followed the seasons gave way to an industrialized, urban life, guided by the clock."[2] In Thoreau's view in the future, "the mass of men lead lives of quiet desperation."[3]

Thoreau, however, offered hope for the future. From his perspective, "solitude and close communion with nature offered more wealth than possesions."[4] He counseled his contemporaries as follows: "I learned from my experiment, if one advances confidently in the direction of his dreams, and endeavors to live the life which he has imagined, he will meet with success unexpected in common hours."[5] This Thoreau quote became the theme upon which Walden University was founded and it underlies the new paradigm of education that emphasizes getting back to the basics and utilizing distance education and remote learning.

During my college days in the 1970s, I always had a typed one-page collection of

Thoreau's quotes pinned on my bulletin board. It included the quote that stated, "I thus found that the student who wishes for a shelter can obtain one for a lifetime at an expense not greater than the rent which he now pays annually."[6] I took this quote to heart and promptly purchased a damaged travel trailer from Flesch Construction for $100 and renovated it for $700, then lived in it during my second year in college for much less in total expenses than I would otherwise have paid for rent.

To reaffirm Thoreau's point, I subsequently built my own home in New Mexico in the 1980s for about $50,000. I close this text with one final Thoreau quote: "If I seem to boast more than is becoming, my excuse is that I boast for humanity rather than for myself; and my shortcomings and inconsistencies do not affect the truth of my statement."[7]

Acknowledgments

I want to extend sincere thanks to all those who assisted me in seeing this short history of Walden come to fruition. People from Walden who helped include Bonnita E. Ary, Gordon Brocker, Rick Cornelison, Jim Dustin, Melanie Leaverton, Rosa Mae Nelson, Paul Willard Richard, Rex Shaw, Carl and Patty Shuler, Matt Shuler, and Helen Williams.

Special thanks also go to the editor of the book, Barbara Scott; publisher, Rebecca Lenzini; graphic designer Ana Karina Armijo for the cover design; and Kris Shaw and Maria Arabella Penner for photos and sketches in the book.

Notes

CHAPTER 1
The Prehistory—Indians Reign Supreme

1. Paul Willard Richard, *Colorado's North Park: History, Wildlife, and Ranching* (Walden Press Inc., 2009) p. 4.
2. Corina A. Santistevan and Julia Moore, eds., *Taos: A Topical History* (Santa Fe, NM: Museum of New Mexico Press, 2013), pp. 27-28.
3. Henry David Thoreau, *Walden* (New York: Barnes & Noble, 2012), p. 142.
4. Ibid. p. 137.
5. Hazel Gresham, *North Park* (Cheyenne, WY: Pioneer Printing, 2006), p. 141.
6. Paul Willard Richard, *Colorado's North Park: History, Wildlife, and Ranching* (Walden Press Inc., 2009) p. 4.

CHAPTER 2
Exploration, Trapping, and Hunting

1. F.R. Bob Romero, *History of Taos* (Taos, NM: F.R. Bob Romero, 2015), pp. 55-56.
2. Hazel Gresham, *North Park* (Cheyenne, WY: Pioneer Printing, 2006), p. 9.
3. Ibid. p. 8.
4. Paul Willard Richard, *Colorado's North Park: History, Wildlife, and Ranching* (Walden Press Inc., 2009), p. 129.

5. Hazel Gresham, *North Park* (Cheyenne, WY: Pioneer Printing, 2006), p. 9.
6. Paul Willard Richard, *Colorado's North Park: History, Wildlife, and Ranching* (Walden Press Inc., 2009), p. 130.
7. Ibid. pp. 4-5.
8. John Nichols, *My Heart Belongs to Nature* (Albuquerque: University of New Mexico Press), p. 10.
9. Paul Willard Richard, *Colorado's North Park: History, Wildlife, and Ranching* (Walden Press Inc., 2009), p. 6.

CHAPTER 3
Early White Settlement

1. Hazel Gresham, *North Park* (Cheyenne, WY: Pioneer Printing, 2006), p. 14.
2. Paul Willard Richard, *Colorado's North Park: History, Wildlife, and Ranching* (Walden Press Inc., 2009), p. 130.
3. Hazel Gresham, *North Park* (Cheyenne, WY: Pioneer Printing, 2006), p. 13.
4. Ibid. p. 13.
5. Ibid. pp. 15-16.
6. Ibid. p. 20.
7. Ibid. p. 38.

CHAPTER 4
Mining and the Founding of Walden

1. Hazel Gresham, *North Park* (Cheyenne, WY: Pioneer Printing, 2006), p. 18.
2. Ibid. pp. 50-51.
3. Paul Willard Richard, *Colorado's North Park: History, Wildlife, and Ranching* (Walden Press Inc., 2009), p. 131.

4. Hazel Gresham, *North Park* (Cheyenne, WY: Pioneer Printing, 2006), p. 67.
5. Ibid. pp. 355-356.
6. *The Jackson County Star* (commemorative edition), "Early Day History of Walden," Pete Lepponen and Tolly Ann Gore, November 8, 1990, p. 14.
7. Ibid. p. 14.
8. Hazel Gresham, *North Park* (Cheyenne, WY: Pioneer Printing, 2006), p. 138.
9. *The Jackson County Star* (commemorative edition), "Early Day History of Walden," Pete Lepponen and Tolly Ann Gore, November 8, 1990, p. 14-15.
10. Hazel Gresham, *North Park* (Cheyenne, WY: Pioneer Printing, 2006), p. 201.
11. Ibid. pp. 202-205.
12. Town of Walden, archival minutes from April 1893 meeting, p. 77.

CHAPTER 5
The Origins of the Cattle Ranching Domain

1. Hazel Gresham, *North Park* (Cheyenne, WY: Pioneer Printing, 2006), p. 64.
2. Ibid. p. 12.
3. *The Jackson County Star* (commemorative edition), "Early Day History of Walden," Pete Lepponen and Tolly Ann Gore, November 8, 1990, p. 3.
4. Paul Willard Richard, *Colorado's North Park: History, Wildlife, and Ranching* (Walden Press Inc., 2009), pp. 40-43.
5. Hazel Gresham, *North Park* (Cheyenne, WY: Pioneer Printing, 2006), p. 109.

6. This author uses the slogan Hub of the Park to describe the significance of Walden's central location and to highlight its historical impact in North Park.
7. Hazel Gresham, *North Park* (Cheyenne, WY: Pioneer Printing, 2006), p. 28.
8. Ibid. p. 65.
9. Will & Deni McIntyre, *Three Ranches* (Winston-Salem, NC: Loose Ends Press, 2012), p. 55.
10. Ibid. p. 3.
11. Stephen Payne, *Where the Rockies Ride Herd* (Stephen Payne, 1965), p. 68.
12. Ibid. p. 69.
13. Hazel Gresham, *North Park* (Cheyenne, WY: Pioneer Printing, 2006), p. 26.
14. Paul Willard Richard, *Colorado's North Park: History, Wildlife, and Ranching* (Walden Press Inc., 2009), p. 13.
15. This information was acquired through an interview conducted in November 2020 with Rosa Mae Nelson, great-granddaughter of John Henry Brocker.
16. Hazel Gresham, *North Park* (Cheyenne, WY: Pioneer Printing, 2006), p. 61.
17. Ibid. p. 81.
18. Ibid. p. 208.
19. Ibid. pp. 106-110.
20. Ibid. p. 111.
21. Ibid. p. 322.
22. Ibid. p. 153.
23. Stephen Payne, *Where the Rockies Ride Herd* (Stephen Payne, 1965), p. 123.
24. Ibid. p. 24.
25. Paul Willard Richard, *Colorado's North Park: History, Wildlife, and Ranching* (Walden Press Inc.,

2009), p. 54.
26. Stephen Payne, *Where the Rockies Ride Herd* (Stephen Payne, 1965), p. 45.
27. Paul Willard Richard, *Colorado's North Park: History, Wildlife, and Ranching* (Walden Press Inc., 2009), p. 56.
28. F.R. Bob Romero, *Roots of Enchantment* (Taos, NM: Nighthawk Press, 2018), p. 49.
29. Hazel Gresham, *North Park* (Cheyenne, WY: Pioneer Printing, 2006), p. 195.
30. Paul Willard Richard, *Colorado's North Park: History, Wildlife, and Ranching* (Walden Press Inc., 2009), p. 116.
31. Will & Deni McIntyre, *Three Ranches* (Winston-Salem, NC: Loose Ends Press, 2012), p. 132.
32. Stephen Payne, *Where the Rockies Ride Herd* (Stephen Payne, 1965), p. 116.
33. Ibid. p. 256.
34. Paul Willard Richard, *Colorado's North Park: History, Wildlife, and Ranching* (Walden Press Inc., 2009), p. 113.
35. Henry David Thoreau, *Walden* (New York: Barnes & Noble, 2012), p. 43.
36. Paul Willard Richard, *Colorado's North Park: History, Wildlife, and Ranching* (Walden Press Inc., 2009), p. 157.
37. Ibid. p. 159.

CHAPTER 6
Early Twentieth Century in Walden

1. Hazel Gresham, *North Park* (Cheyenne, WY: Pioneer Printing, 2006), p. 140.
2. Ibid. p. 326.
3. Ibid. p. 207.

4. *The Jackson County Star* (commemorative edition), "Early Day History of Walden," Pete Lepponen and Tolly Ann Gore, Nov. 8, 1990, pp. 16-18. Also refer to Hazel Gresham, *North Park,* p. 340.
5. Ibid. p. 17.
6. Hazel Gresham, *North Park* (Cheyenne, WY: Pioneer Printing, 2006), p. 120. Also refer to Stephen Payne, *Where the Rockies Ride Herd,* p. 277.
7. Ibid. p. 120
8. Ibid. p. 340.
9. Ibid. p. 340.
10. Stephen Payne, *Where the Rockies Ride Herd* (Stephen Payne, 1965), p. 277.
11. Hazel Gresham, *North Park* (Cheyenne, WY: Pioneer Printing, 2006), p. 364.
12. Stephen Payne, *Where the Rockies Ride Herd* (Stephen Payne, 1965), p. 285.
13. Hazel Gresham, *North Park* (Cheyenne, WY: Pioneer Printing, 2006), pp. 82-85.
14. Ibid. p. 85.
15. Ibid. p. 364.
16. Ibid. pp. 364-365.
17. *The Jackson County Star* (commemorative edition), "Early Day History of Walden," Pete Lepponen and Tolly Ann Gore, November 8, 1990, p. 19. Also refer to Gresham, *North Park,* pp. 367-368.
18. Hazel Gresham, *North Park* (Cheyenne, WY: Pioneer printing, 2006), p. 367.
19. Ibid. p. 367-368.
20. Ibid. p. 378.

21. *The Jackson County Star* (commemorative edition), "Early Day History of Walden," Pete Lepponen and Tolly Ann Gore, November 8, 1990, p. 19.
22. Hazel Gresham, North Park (Cheyenne, WY: Pioneer Printing, 2006), p. 379.
23. Ibid. p. 378.
24. Ibid. pp. 370-371.
25. *The Jackson County Star,* "Walden Editor Shot by Enraged Citizen," May 14, 2020, p. 4., and the May 6, 1910, edition of the *Grand Encampment Herald.*

CHAPTER 7
The Local Employment/Industries—Government, Education, Mining, Timber, Gas and Oil, Railroad, Retail, Outdoor Recreation, and Tourism

1. *The Jackson County Star,* "Jackson County Chronicles," September 12, 2019, p. 4.
2. Hazel Gresham, *North Park* (Cheyenne, WY: Pioneer Printing, 2006), p. 196.
3. Ibid. pp. 196-197.
4. Ibid. pp. 196-197.
5. *The Jackson County Star* (commemorative edition), "Early Day History of Walden," Pete Lepponen and Tolly Ann Gore, November 8, 1990. p. 6. Also refer to *The Jackson County Star,* "Report of Fluorspar Reserve in Northgate Area," February 17, 1944, pp. 1-2.
6. Some information about Fluorspar mining in North Park was obtained via telephone interview with Rex Shaw in December 2020.

7. *The Jackson County Star* (commemorative edition), "Early Day History of Walden," Pete Lepponen and Tolly Ann Gore, November 8, 1990, p. 8.
8. Hazel Gresham, *North Park* (Cheyenne, WY: Pioneer Printing, 2006), p. 331.
9. Earlene Belew Bradley, *Timber Times and Tales, An Early History of Gould, Colorado* (LaPorte, CO: Earlene Belew Bradley, 2006), p. 9.
10. Ibid. p. 25.
11. Ibid. p. 51.
12. Ibid. p. 51.
13. Ibid. p. 8.
14. Ibid. p. 26.
15. *The Jackson County Star*, "Jackson County Chronicles," July 4, 2019, p. 4.
16. Paul Willard Richard, *Colorado's North Park: History, Wildlife, and Ranching* (Walden Press Inc., 2009), pp. 155-156.

CHAPTER 8

The Future of Walden:
Assumptions, New Trends, and Potential

1. *The Jackson County Star*, "Internet Is Down Again, a Problem" (Matt Shuler Editorial), December 3, 2020, p. 2.
2. F.R. Bob Romero, *Roots of Enchantment* (Taos, NM, Nighthawk Press, 2018), pp. 18-19.
3. Hazel Gresham, *North Park* (Cheyenne, WY: Pioneer Printing, 2006), p. 338.
4. Paul Willard Richard, *Colorado's North Park: History, Wildlife, and Ranching* (Walden Press Inc., 2009), p. 160.
5. Ibid. p. 160.

Afterword

1. Henry David Thoreau, *Walden* (New York: Barnes & Noble, 2012), p. xii.
2. Ibid. p. xiii.
3. Ibid. p. xiv.
4. Ibid. p. xiv.
5. Ibid. p. 250.
6. Ibid. p. 38.
7. Ibid. p. 38.

Suggested Reading List

Bradley, Earlene Belew
Timber Times and Tales

Gresham, Hazel
North Park

McIntyre, Will & Deni
Three Ranches

Payne, Stephen
Where the Rockies Ride Herd

Richard, Paul Willard
Colorado's North Park:
History, Wildlife, and Ranching

Thoreau, Henry David
Walden

Mayors

March 2, 1891-April 2, 1894	C.E. Mosman
April 3, 1894-April 2, 1895	P.W. Fischer
April 3, 1895-April 4, 1898	C.E. Mosman
April 5, 1898-April 17, 1899	P.W. Fischer

(by one vote over K.J. MacCallum)

April 18, 1899-April 16, 1900	K.J. MacCallum
April 17, 1900-April 14, 1902	C.E. Mosman
April 15, 1902-April 19, 1904	Harry L. Baugh
April 20, 1904-April 20, 1908	A.E. Butler
April 21, 1908-April 19, 1909	C.E. Mosman
April 20, 1909-Feb. 17, 1910	P.W. Fischer
Feb. 18, 1910-April 18, 1910	A.A. Hunter (Acting)
April 19, 1910-April 19, 1911	W.O. Mosman
April 20, 1911-Nov. 1912	Harry Green
Nov. 1912-Nov. 1916	K.J. MacCallum
Nov. 1916-Nov. 1923	E.N. Butler
Nov. 1923-Nov. 1927	J.K.P. McCallum
Nov. 1927-Nov. 1931	C.E. Mosman
Nov. 1931-Nov. 1937	Carlos C. Case
Nov. 1937-Nov. 1938	W.F. Hill
Nov. 1938-Nov. 1944	Archie G. Maine
Nov. 1944-Nov. 1950	Victor I. Riley

Nov. 1950-Nov. 1956	Peter H. Lepponen
Nov. 1956-Nov. 1959	Russel Crowder
Nov. 1959-Nov. 1960	James C. Pitcher
Nov. 1960-Jan. 1961	John C. Chedsey
Jan. 1962-April 1964	M.E. Hauptman
April 1964-April 15, 1968	H.E. Berry
April 16, 1968-April 20, 1970	Harold Dodge Jr.
April 21, 1970-April 22, 1974	William J. Porterfield
April 23, 1974-April 17, 1978	James H. Shawver
April 18, 1978-April 11, 1982	John H. Gresham
April 12, 1982-April 27, 1986	Joan Follett
April 28, 1986-April 22, 1990	Richard F. Wyatt
April 23, 1990-April 10, 1994	Barbara J. Hughes
April 11, 1994-April 12, 1998	Naida L. Crowner
April 13, 1998-April 2006	Kyle Fliniau
April 2006-April 2009	Dirk Ramsey
April 2009-April 2010	Carol Purcell (Mayor Pro Tem, Acting)
April 2010-April 2014	James H. Carothers
April 2014-August 2014	Kyle Fliniau
August 2014-Present	Jim Dustin

Walden Pond Poem
By Henry David Thoreau

It is no dream of mine,
To ornament a line;
I cannot come nearer to God and Heaven
Than I live to Walden even.
I am its stony shore,
And the breeze that passes o'er:
In the hollow of my hand
Are its water and its sand,
And its deepest resort
Lies high in my thought.

I Am from Walden
By F.R. Bob Romero

I am from Walden!
A place up in the Rockies high.
A town in north central Colorado, hark!
Walden is the heart and Hub of North Park.

The spirit of the first Americans still lives;
In the land, the water, and the air.
The Indians hunted bison, drank the water,
 and they fared well.
The European explorers, mountain men,
 and miners tried, and they survived.
The resilient and resolute cattle ranchers
 then arrived.
They left their footprint and some even
 thrived.
The lumberjacks, roughnecks, merchants,
 and railroad hands did their share;
All came, and most made a good living there.

The people who live in Walden are survivors.
For they are hardy, tough, tenacious, and vigilant.
The Waldenite ancestors' stock was all immigrant!
Their descendants' hybrid vigor will persevere;
For they all have endured Walden winters, severe!
From throughout the country and the world they did hail.
And in life and eternity they will prevail.
I am from Walden!

www.ingramcontent.com/pod-product-compliance
Lightning Source LLC
Chambersburg PA
CBHW020909090426
42736CB00008B/551